FIND

Desmond Knipe

Table of Contents

Foreword 1

Copyrights 2

Why do religions and beliefs differ? 3

MEDITATION 6

COMMUNICATION 11

LISTENING 15

Energy Topics and Divining Tools 21

REQUESTING 30

How Do You View the World? 33

How Would You Like to be Treated? 39

Healing Yourself and Others 42

What Happens When We Die? 46

How Do You Want Your World to Look? 49

In its purest form, meditation simply connects your body and spirit with the Divine cosmos, this allows for the transfer of understandings, from past, present, and future, within this dimension and others.

Foreword

This is an expansion of my first book FIX IT, A basic guide to your spiritual health. Where my first book covered the basics on various topics, this book delves deeper into the aspects of the topics and provides an expanded understanding.

I will cover a little more of the roles that some of the practices, such as meditation, have played throughout human history, provide more pathways of understanding, and go a little deeper into the how to.

By the end of this book, you will have the confidence and understanding to assist others with their spiritual awakenings, divine messages from various sources, and conduct energy healings.

Unlike my previous book, FIX IT, A basic guide to your spiritual health, which is basically a wakeup call for some, and a very basic user's manual for connecting with your higher self, for others, this book will reveal a deeper understanding of each topic. You do not need to completely understand every part of each, just the parts the resonate with you.

Copyrights

Copyright © 2021 by Desmond Knipe

All rights reserved.

No portion of this book may be reproduced in any form without written permission from the publisher or author, except as permitted by U.S. copyright law.

This publication is designed to provide accurate and authoritative information in regard to the subject matter covered. It is sold with the understanding that neither the author nor the publisher is engaged in rendering legal, investment, accounting or other professional services. While the publisher and author have used their best efforts in preparing this book, they make no representations or warranties with respect to the accuracy or completeness of the contents of this book and specifically disclaim any implied warranties of merchantability or fitness for a particular purpose. No warranty may be created or extended by sales representatives or written sales materials. The advice and strategies contained herein may not be suitable for your situation. You should consult with a professional when appropriate. Neither the publisher nor the author shall be liable for any loss of profit or any other commercial damages, including but not limited to special, incidental, consequential, personal, or other damages.

Book Cover by Brendan Bowdan

Edition Number 2 edition Published 2024

Why do religions and beliefs differ?

Throughout humanity's history there have been, what we refer to as intuitive people, these people had the ability to connect through spirit, to the Divine cosmos, where they connected with beings that, for our tiny little human brains, were not comprehensible, so, as most human beings do, they put them into groups that were already understood as being more than the description or name that they were given, Gods, Angels, Aliens, and the like.

In the very early days this was how the gods came about, many religions were created to follow entities that we called gods, but they were just messengers, guides, angels, and the like, that were simply giving that person's higher self/spirit a nudge/ reminder of the path they should be following.

These intuitive humans would sometimes go on to explain the message or messages that they had received whilst in communication with these entities, and as you can imagine, if they were unable to understand that these entities were not the universal power, then the message's that they would try to translate, lost a lot in the translation. Not to mention the individuals own ability to articulate correctly, the information that had been passed to them.

Then of course we need to add to this, story, or message decay, much like Chinese whispers, the story would lose much of its original meaning, and become embellished in other areas, as it passed from generation to generation.

With the invention of recording systems, cave paintings, carvings, and eventually written language, the story decay of course lessened, and was replaced by mankind's corruption. At some stage someone worked out that if they controlled the narrative of the god's writings, then they were all powerful, in their society.

During mankind's time on our little planet, a few have always looked to control the many, whether that was through war, village hierarchy, religion, business, basically any form of organisation that could install fear or greed in the masses. This is still happening today.

Now if we consider the modern-day religions, in many ways some have grown and adapted with the growth of humanity and humanity's understanding of the universe, and others still try to hold to all the beliefs that were translated from their so-called holy scriptures, I will apologise here to anyone that still has the belief that their scriptures have been written by god, and that there has absolutely been no human interference with these scriptures in the centuries since they were first revealed.

Although we still must factor in all the above information for all these religions, the fundamental messages that come from all these different religions, their stories, are similar, if not the same.

There is one God. Remember that what many referred to as gods, were messengers.

You should not use god's name, but for God alone.

You should create time for worship regularly.

You should do good things to for your elders, look after them.

You should not kill one another.

You should not screw around or take advantage of anyone for sex.

You should not steal from one another.

You should not lie, as to incriminate another.

You should not be jealous, of others, their property, or their status.

You should look out for each other, help one another, treat others as you would have them treat you.

You should take care of your body as it is your temple.

There is a lot more that we could list here, but I think you get what I am saying, so, let us imagine for a moment, that everyone on our planet lived this way, if you only conducted yourself to help others improve their life and they in turn were looking to improve yours and others. How would that look, how would that feel.

You would of course have the negative people, the nay Sayers, resisting at the start, but I do believe that once they could see the benefits to their life and their family's lives, they would become positive as well.

I would like you to take some time to lament on this thought, and we shall return to it later in this book.

Let us take a look at a key element in treating your body as a temple, shall we?

MEDITATION

I would just like to take the time to acknowledge you, the reader. There is something great happening on our planet at the moment and I am so pleased that you have chosen to be a part of it.

Some archaeologists date meditation back to early 5000 BCE, and the practice itself has religious ties in ancient Egypt and China, as well as Hinduism, Judaism, and Buddhism, just to name a few.

Meditation's global spread began along the Silk Road about five or six centuries BCE, as the practice moved throughout Asia, it would arrive in a new spot, then it would slowly transform to fit each new culture. But it really was not until the 20th century that it moved beyond the realm of specific religions, especially in the West.

Many forms of meditation have been developed throughout the years and this allows us access to a plethora of styles that we can use, as is, or change to suit, or ever combine to allow for different results.

"In its purest form, meditation simply connects your body and spirit with the Divine cosmos, this allows for the transfer of understandings, from past, present, and future, within this dimension and others. As we all interpret things in different ways, and our understandings, when it comes to the Divine cosmos, are limited, this means that there is a lot lost in the translation." (Channelled from a spirit guide)

Many meditations have been channelled, meaning that a person has gained knowledge via their higher self, developed their interpretation of this information, and passed it on to others. So, if we can just look at something that holds true for all of us, one shoe will not fit everyone, then we start to understand that for all the different types, and styles of meditation, we only need to find the one that fits us the best.

I will now explain some of the more well-known meditation practices, then I will channel one or two, specifically for this book, if none of the meditations that follow, resonate with you, then please start looking for the ones that do. Internet, books, connections on earth and in spirit, if you have read Fix it, a basic guide to your spiritual health, then you know where I am going with this suggestion.

1.Mindfulness meditations are basically any form of meditation that involves being aware or present with whatever you are doing, such as brushing your teeth, washing your body, or even just breathing. It is simply being mindful of everything that is taking place. I will lump focused meditation in here as well, as they are similar. Focused meditation is where you focus your mind on something, whether that be your breathing, a certain point of focus for your eyes, such as a dot, or picturing something in your mind to focus on. Many would-be meditators lose a lot of sleep attempting to keep their minds focused and fail so many times that meditation goes straight into that to-hard-to-do basket. Mindfulness and Focused meditations are very simple to do, when your mind wanders, and it will, you simply go back to what you were meditating on, if you simply remember the successes, and not the failures, these are two of the easiest types of meditation for beginners, it just takes time.

2.Mantra meditations are when some very basic words or sounds are repeated, over and over and over again. The sounds of "so" on an inward breath, and "hum" on an outward breath work just as well when you replace them with "in" and "out," or "up" and "down." These are normally said inside the mind, or in a whisper, whilst focusing on your breathing.

Mantra meditations have become primarily connected with the chanting's we hear from many monks within monasteries around the world, in different religions or sects, although these meditations are more chanting meditation, rather that mantra.

3.Spiritual meditation takes many forms, the two formerly mentioned and others including prayer, light, and sound meditations. The main focus is for the person to connect with spirit, God, the divine being, the universal power. This practice has been taking place on earth for centuries, depending on who you were attempting to connect with, you would be considered a holy person, or a witch, and many other things in-between. It is my understanding that no matter if you are attempting to connect to God, angels, the universal power, the old gods, for the Wiccan's and witches, Gia -mother earth, we are all attempting to connect with the same thing, as my guide put it earlier, the Divine cosmos.

4.Movement meditations are a vast array of meditations involving different body movements, from yoga, tai-chi to even just walking. The idea is that as you focus on the task that your body is moving to, you make a conscious effort to be aware of your surroundings but centre your mind and body, make them one with your surroundings. In some of these, there are combinations of movement and Mantra meditations.

5.Technology meditations, science has conducted a great deal of research into meditation, the benefits, both physical and emotional, they have mapped the human brain and found that it responds to various stimuli. Music, sound, various drugs, and many more avenues have been discovered in an attempt to make it easier for humans to feel the connection that is achieved through meditation. For some people the connection they create using these methods work for them. I would just like to say here that inducing meditation via drugs, although it has been done for centuries, is probably not the best avenue for most of you. The old ways used all-natural inducements, whereas many of the drugs available over the counter, or through illegal channels can be very detrimental to our delicate brain.

Throughout all these meditations, they bring centring, physical changes to your body, in the form of relaxation, lowing the heart rate and blood pressure, in most cases. On a spiritual level, this centring allows for our connection with spirit/God/the Divine Cosmos to become focused, this connection is always there, but by meditating we can create clearer communication lines.

By creating clearer communication with our higher selves, we are enabled to gain a better understanding of what our higher self wants to achieve on this plane, messages are more precise, relevant and we can ask questions if things are unclear to our human brain. This connection is the portal that allows for Astral projection and many other things that I will not get into here, yet, basically the better this connection is kept, the better your communication will be.

Here are two very quick meditations;

1.Pressure – With your eyes closed and breathing noted, squeeze the tips of your thumb and index fingers together, on both hands to create pressure, make sure it is forceful. As you feel the sensation from the pressure moving up your arms, through your neck, and lower jaw, in your mind, see the fog, or dark clouds above you blocking the portal/window to your higher self. Then release the pressure from your thumb and finger, on both hands, in your mind see the fog, or dark clouds move aside to reveal the portal/window to you. Focus on the portal/window, ask questions, and listen for the answers, enjoy your conversations with yourself. When you have finished, tell yourself that by the count of five you will be wide awake and refreshed.

2.Sensing – This is for the people who have experienced the connection before but still struggle to connect on a consistent basis. With your eyes closed and breathing noted, simply go to the place in your mind that you believe the portal/window is, ask your higher self for the guidance to locate it, and slowly start moving your mind focus around that vicinity, when you find it, you will receive a very clear picture in your mind. Now that picture might not be of the portal/window, it may not be a picture, it may be a sound, or anything, but you will know. Feel in your mind where you received this and you will always have a point of reference to go to, even without meditation.

Once you have established your connection to your higher self you can access that connection without needing to meditate. However, please continue to practice meditation as it is very good for your body, soul, and planet. The energies that are moved as part of our meditation, aura cleansing, grounding process, reinvigorate the earths energies, and the more of us that practice this, the healthier those energies become.

Your higher-self will guide you to this but it is good to take an hour or two each month to enhance your connection, just meditate and allow your higher-self to guide you.

For anyone still struggling with meditation, you are not alone, please investigate your breathing. This was extremely helpful for me, breathing in through my nose for a count of 3 or 4, holding that breath for a count of 3 or 4, then exhaling through my mouth for a count of 3 or 4. I would do this for as long as I felt I needed to, then revert to my normal breathing, and conduct the meditation I had set out to do.

You simply need to find what will work for you, get on the internet, read books, find a mentor, do the work to find out what it is that really works for you.

COMMUNICATION

What an interesting concept, communication with God, the angels, spirit guides, as well as humans. We are about to go into the unknown, or so some think, to retrieve answers that cannot be true, as if they were, they may prove the existence of God, a higher power, the Divine Cosmos.

How we as humans communicate with the Divine Cosmos varies with regard to our beliefs, if you are a Muslim, you pray to Allah, if you are a Christian, you pray to God, or Jesus, the Jews, YHWH, it is spirit for the new age, and so the list goes on. Let us just put all of these into a box with the same phone number and understand that we are all trying to contact the same thing.

One of the biggest hurdle's that we humans face is that most of us have no idea how to comprehend anything that the Divine Cosmos may want to impart to us directly, if it elected to do so. Therefore, it is mostly our spiritual selves that receive information from the Divine Cosmos, and pass it on to us, and our spiritual selves intern make sure that our prayers/heart felt needs get through to the Divine Cosmos.

Now maybe I have moved ahead too fast for some of you, I will slow it down and let us look at the prayer system, ask for it and it shall be given, seek it and it shall be found, knock and it shall open, pretty simple instructions if you ask me. There are different versions of these in most religions but they are all very similar.

I know many people, as do you, that all they need to do is pray for what they need, and somehow it turns up in their life, or something that would work even better. Most of the time it has been for things that would not only assist the person who is praying, but also others. The point I am making is that this is proof of concept, the system works for some, so how do we get it working for us?

Most of the people I know, that are able to do the above, have a clear communication line with the Divine Cosmos. They can receive assistance to manifest their needs on this plane of existence. I have noticed this with Christians, Muslims, and New Age, you will also know people from different religions, races, and walks of life, that are able to do this as well.

I do need to get this out of the way here, if it does not matter what religion you are from for this to work, then there must be another explanation, right?

If you look closely at these people, study them, start to understand them, you will see that their belief in what they are doing, their belief in their God, religion, basically their communication channel, is strong and clear. They work from their hearts, they know that what they are doing is right, and in their minds, righteous. Many of the worlds business leaders do this as well, we all wonder, why they are so lucky, why do they succeed. Take a look at their belief system, and internal communication.

You might ask, does that mean that If I just believe then I can have whatever I want? The simple answer is no.

We are all capable of manifesting almost anything that our hearts desire, on this plane, unfortunately, most people do not know what their hearts truly desire, as this is connected directly to our higher selves' purpose of being involved on this plane of existence.

Now if we boil all this down into a bite size chunk of information, we then see that as long as what we are requesting is in line with our higher self's purpose, our true life's path, this strengthens our internal belief system, which, as long as our communication channels, both internal and spiritual, are clear, then we should be capable of manifesting whatever our hearts desire.

So, to make this happen in your life, the first step is to make sure that our communication channels are clear. When you connect spiritually, with your higher self, the understanding that you gain enhances your internal communication with yourself.

Some of you reading this already have very clear communication channels with the Divine Cosmos, whether that has been attained through meditation and connection with your higher self, prayer, and God (via, your higher self), or any other way, you have made this connection. Others are still lost, so here are a few things you can do to improve your communication.

1.Meditate daily – Meditation can be conducted in many ways as explained in Chapter 2, but understand that if you have been practicing your religion and praying, then that is also a form of meditation, do not change anything that you feel is right for you. You can add to it, play with it, try new things, find out what makes your communication work better for you, and of course, please listen for the answers. So many people think that meditation or praying is just one way, listen, see, sense, feel, you know communication travels in both directions, do not ignore the information coming back to you.

2.Request help – Your higher self will do as you request if that request will serve you, request clearer communication, this is called helping yourself. I have seen dramatic improvement in others communication just by them taking this step. Request to others for help, this may not be as effective, as what another does for their communication may not work for you, and also how they articulate that information to you may not be the same way that they intend for you to interpret it.

3.Build belief – Start communicating with others that have good internal communication currently, you know who they are, they make things happen for their lives, they get results that make others wonder, how? Ask questions of these people and listen to their replies, the people that do not take credit for the successes themselves are especially the ones you are looking to learn from. They will say things like, with Gods help, through the universal power, and even things like, it was a team effort, my employees made it happen. Many of these people have created a connection with their higher selves, that some are not even aware of, the results that have come from this connection have reinforced their own belief system.

I hope I have not upset too many people with the statements I have made so far, there is a lot to take in, and if I were to pussyfoot around, this book would be way too long, and it would not shock you into the new understanding that you need to have.

Let us move onto the next chapter, Listening.

LISTENING

Most of us know how to listen, even the deaf, I am not kidding. The deaf just listen differently from people who can hear the sounds, from their ears, in their minds. They are more aware of the other senses and utilise them to hear their world, sight, smell, and feel, the reason I have used the word feel here is that touch does not cover it. Feel can encompass many things from touch, vibration, temperature, to sense (I had a feeling).

Some of you already know where I am going with this. When we listen in our world, we hear a sound with our ears, that sound is picked up as vibration, it is then sent to our brain to interpret, we are then able to use our other senses to confirm or deny our interpretation.

Listening to our higher selves, for some is next to impossible, as even their own internal communication is full of doubt, I cannot believe what I heard, I cannot believe what I saw, and so on. For others it is a matter of understanding that hearing does not necessarily have to be auditory, and others yet, upon reading the above have just figured out what they have been missing.

Your communication with your higher self takes place on a regular basis, in many of us it is persistent, as we choose to ignore what is being communicated, for others, **IT**, our ego, just puts it straight into the to-hard-to-understand-basket and we forget about it.

Listening to your higher self is like understanding a new language, please note I have used the word understanding and not learning, this is important. Our higher self has been communicating with us since we were children, you have already learnt this language, all that is left, is to understand.

Now for the fun part. Understanding the information that is passed to your human body via your higher self is not difficult to do, but for many it will take some practice.

1. Confirm and accept that this is Divine communication. As your communication will be specific to you, how your human body can best receive and interpret this information, your internal belief system will require validation, that this indeed is divine communication. As this will differ from the way other people communicate, you must confirm the information you are receiving, for yourself.

1a. Some will hear, you will have a voice in your head, or even many voices. When you have clear communication with your higher self the voice you should listen to will be clear. You will know it is your higher self as everything it relays to you will come from love, not fear or greed, in your heart the communication will ring true for you, not create doubt. When I hear from my higher self, the voice comes to me with a soft pleasant sound and I can sense in my brain where the voice is. The voice of my ego, or **IT**, emanates from a slightly different part of my brain.

1b. Some will see, you will see with your eyes or your mind, and there is a myriad of things that we can be shown, so here is a brief explanation, please understand that sight is not limited to just these. With your eyes open you may see, in full sight, partial (how we envisage seeing a ghost), or even in our mind (the image you see with your eyes stays the same, but what appears in your mind is more). You may see still pictures, as my mother did, she always knew if it was from the divine cosmos as the frames that she would see around each picture were astoundingly beautiful. You may see moving pictures, full life images, colours, patterns, the point is you may be shown anything. When I see, it is mainly in my mind, again, I sense the part of my brain that is receiving this information is different to that of my imagination. One thing I have noticed is when I get these images, they are prominent, they come to the forefront of my mind.

1c. Some will feel, you will feel (sense) pain that another may have, joy, sadness, sorrow, any sensation that our human body is capable of having, you will be able to sense. When I feel, most times it is when I am helping someone, but I do recall a time when I was astral travelling and entered a blackhole, the sensation was to say the least, out-of-this-world, I felt my astral body folding in on itself in all possible ways.

1d. Some will just know, I mean truly know the answer to many things, you will know how to do things that you have had no prior knowledge of. You may have Deja Vue, premonitions, the feeling that you have done it before. When I know, I just let my mind and body do what they do, the words come out and my body acts, but it is more like I am in the passenger seat, I am aware and could stop it if I choose to. The answers, the truths, that come of this just resonate with my heart.

1e. Some will have a combination, you will see and hear, or feel and know, or a combination of them all. As you probably picked up through my explanations, I have experienced them all, as can you. We are capable of all of these.

Once you have identified how you listen to your higher self, you can now confirm this by asking your higher self for that conformation, then your human brain can now accept this to be true. Once you have done this you will have proven the existence of God, to yourself, and that is all that truly matters.

2. Practice. When you understand how you listen to your higher self, you will increase your internal belief and communication, practice, listen, ask questions, and start to understand what information is coming to you and how.

Be aware, you will find that there is normally more than one form of communication coming in, it is us that miss these other communication forms, as we become dependent on the form of listening that we are accustomed to.

3. Understand. This is best if I explain how I understand first, here are some examples.

3a. I was driving down a gravel road one day, in a very large, Kenworth truck. The road was narrow, as it was a back road in farming country, it was dusty, undulating, and had many bends. I was traveling at speed and driving up one of the many hills, when a picture of a cow entered my head, in the place that I normally received information from my higher self, this image then went straight to the forefront of my mind. I automatically started to slow my truck down. As I crossed the crest of the hill, I saw a cow, in the middle of the road, the cow was standing still, looking at my truck. As I had previously started to slow down, I had enough time to come to a stop and blast my air horn to get the cow moving. If I had not slowed down, as I did prior to going over the crest, the cow and the truck would have been a mess.

3b. This has happened far too many times for me to leave it out of this book. Many times, in my life I have seen, and felt, people in physical pain, I would often choose to ignore these feelings when they first started happening, I now know better. I now, always ask the person if they are ok, to which the reply is almost always "no," then I ask them if I can help, as I am able to conduct energy healing. If the answer is "yes," this is where I have learnt to take the passenger seat. I am normally able to find the issue connected with their pain in 10 to 20 seconds, I have found that most of my healings are conducted on the persons back with pressure points. I have no training in pressure points, I am just guided to put pressure on points, it can be soft or hard, depending on how I am guided. Most people have instant relief from their pain, for some it may take a

FIND IT, THE NEXT STEP IN YOUR SPIRITUAL HEALTH

day or two, but if that is the case, I am normally given that message to pass on to them.

3c. I have only started doing this for this very book. I asked my higher self for assistance in writing this book, six days ago. I was introduced to a guide, this guide came to me in an internal vision, with internal conversation, the assistance and connection have been amazing for me. The area of assistance so far, has come in the form of, Divine Cosmos knowledge, intimate understanding of humanity and our higher selves, and the ability to articulate these understandings in a way that can be understood by humanity. The way this happens, I can only describe as a combination of a. and b. I request assistance from my higher self, get a picture of this guide in my head, ask the guide to assist with knowledge or articulation, I receive a type of download of information on the topic, then basically take the passenger seat. I am still in control and I am able to change the wording or direction of the writing, but the information being channelled to these pages is not all from me, but it is through me.

Understand. That is a big ask right, for years you have been wondering why you were born, what was the meaning of life, is there a God. Now you hear that the answers to them all are inside you, surly not, right?

Once you have established your main area of listening, right now, confirmed and accepted that, practiced, as to develop your internal belief, then began to understand the messages that are being given to your human brain via your higher self, you will start to understand it all. It will no longer feel foreign, you will start to become bilingual, or multilingual.

Once you know how to listen to the Divine Cosmos, you are then able to ask for the assistance you require, to manifest your needs, goals, dreams, here on earth.

Before we move on to requesting, I have been guided to cover energy topics and divining tools, as some people may require the use of these until they have the confidence with their internal belief to accept that they are able to communicate in other ways with the Divine Cosmos.

Energy Topics and Divining Tools

Science has attempted, and from my understanding science is still attempting, to confirm the existence of what we refer to as Divine energy, Aura, Chakras, grounding cords, basically any form of energy that many ancient and modern religions, sects, and people, believe are connected with the human body.

In 1939, Semyon Davidovich Kirlian, discovered that if he sent an electrical charge though a photo that was to be developed, it would produce a glowing contour around the object that had been photographed, some have proposed that these images show levels of psychic powers and bio-energies.

However, scientific studies have found that the Kirlian effect is caused by the presence of moisture, on the object being photographed. Electricity produces an area of gas ionization around the object if it is moist, which is the case for living things. This causes an alternation of the electric charge pattern on the film. Do not you love how science can explain this away.

So, if we apparently cannot take a photograph of these energies, not everyone can see these energies, and science cannot prove the existence of these energies, how do we know that they are there?

I do not know if you can recall drawing as a child but I distinctly remember drawing pictures of people with rainbows around them, I have seen this repeated by other children throughout my life.

I met a lady that thought everyone was able to see auras, as she had seen them all her life, and it was not until her and her husband saw a stall for Kirlian Photography, at a local market, that she worked out that not everyone could see as she did.

Here is the long story in short, as you have previously worked out, you can communicate with the Divine Cosmos, you simply have to approach this in a different manner to humanities channels of communication with each other.

The same can be said for our spiritual energies, these energies are best viewed as a part of the Divine Cosmos, which of course science is still unable to detect, you can view these energies in some of the ways I have explained in Chapter 4, Listening. When you start with your own energies first, you gain the belief, then you will start to recognise other energies around you.

Throughout humanities development on the earth plane, our spiritual selves or guides, beings that have delivered messages from the Divine Cosmos, have bought in messages of the energies that are connected to our bodies, to other living things, and our world, with the understanding that at some stage in humanities development this information would be utilised for further growth, spiritually.

Well maybe that time is now. Following is something that you are all capable of doing at this moment. As you develop your skills, your internal belief will build and you will discover new and different ways to do these and other things.

Sensing, cleansing, grounding, and protecting your aura I have covered in my previous book, so if you do not understand how to do them yet maybe get your hands on that.

Utilising what you have just read about communication and listening from the previous two chapters, you are going to ask your higher self to show you or allow yourself to see your aura.

Once that is in your mind, in the spot that you know you receive your divine communication, your divine spot. Take note of how it looks, the colours, any dark areas, or areas of disruption, if it looks healthy to you.

FIND IT, THE NEXT STEP IN YOUR SPIRITUAL HEALTH

If you feel you require cleansing, go ahead, if not just study your aura, see the colours, the shape, feel it, how does it feel to you, take note of any smells or tastes. What are the strong characteristics that you can pick up or sense, where and how do you receive the most information?

When you have finished the above, find another living being, plant, animal, or human, and using what you have discovered about your own aura, ask your higher self to allow yourself to view the aura of that being. Again, ensure that you are receiving the information in your divine spot, take note of the aura, if it is healthy, that is great, just take note of what you are seeing. If not, ask the beings higher self if you can assist with an aura cleansing. If the answer is "yes" you can do to that aura, what you would do to cleanse your own aura. If the answer is "no," just take note of what you are seeing.

Whilst conducting the above exercise, you can view the being's protection and grounding, you will also be able to see, or become aware of, any psychic hooks, if any of those areas seem as though they would benefit from your help, simply ask if you can assist in those areas, and listen for the answer.

Chakras, where to start? Do we start with the emergence of the idea of two separate bodies, subtle body (Spiritual body) and physical body form India, within Hinduism, Buddhism, and other religions? Maybe how the chakras are classed as energy centres in the Chinese practice of acupuncture, but do not have a precise physical connection to the body?

I think I will let our guide help us out again.

"The Chakra system is simply the points at which divine energy has the closest contact to the physical form that we are manifesting on this plane. When we become aware of these points of contact, and can strengthen them, we are not only able to rectify or enhance our physical being, but also attract a much stronger ability of manifestation, related to each point."

Well, there you have it, for some readers the Chakra system has now just made sense, for others it is as clear as mud, and others yet may need to unlearn what they have learnt. The interesting thing that I have discovered with channelling some of this information is that I am left with an understanding of the topic that was just not there previously. Let us dig a little deeper, shall we?

Chakras Colour Affecting in Alignment Not aligned

3rd Eye Purple Awareness Attentive Oblivious

Throat Blue Communication Openness Subdued

Heart Green Love/Healing Love Anger

Solar Plexus Yellow Wisdom/Power Confidence Feeble

Sacral Orange Creativity/Sexuality Innovation Blocked

Root Red Trust/Energy Certainty Doubt

Using this basic chart above, you should be able to see if you need to align any of your Chakras. If you still do not trust what you are being shown by your higher self, look at the last two columns of this graph, work out if your chakras are in alignment or not, then do the following exercise. If you have developed the trust then just follow along.

Again, utilising what you have read previously, regarding communication and listening, you are going to ask your higher self to show you or to allow yourself to see your chakra system. Once you have the chakra system in your mind, again in your divine spot, start to notice the size of the energy centres, are they all they same size, are they different shapes?

FIND IT, THE NEXT STEP IN YOUR SPIRITUAL HEALTH

Are they all spinning the same way, are they all spinning? Look at their colours, look at their cleanliness, do you need to cleanse them?

When I clean my balls, my energy balls that is, I use the same process that I use for my aura. I call on the light of cleansing from the city of light, I see it enter through my crown chakra, and then continue through each chakra. This can also come from behind each chakra individually, or all at the same time, depending on what is best for you. Whilst this is taking place I will re-size any chakra that is not consistent, I do this in my mind, blow into the chakra to make it bigger, or pull, or push it into shape or size, mentally.

Once you sense that your chakras are clean, you can call the individual colours for each chakra, call on the chakra rainbow, anything that communicates to the divine cosmos that you are looking to invigorate your energy centres, chakras. As the chakras are receiving this light, you can also ensure that they are spinning, or spinning in the correct direction, at the correct speed. Remember, if you are unsure, ask your higher self for guidance.

If there is an area in your life, that you have noted, requiring specific attention, let us say you are easily angered. Then make sure that after the above process is completed, focus just on your Heart chakra. When I focus on an individual chakra, I see it as one of those glass balls that spins atop a small water fountain, and has internal lighting as it spins.

Everything that you have done for your chakra system, you can now do for this one chakra, focus on it, see it in your mind, feel the power connected to it, make sure it is clean, no blemishes, the colour is bright and vibrant, it is the correct size, and spinning the correct way. As you do all of this be aware of what other images, smells, sounds, or feelings are coming through, these may be challenges in your life that need to be addressed or rectified.

Understanding that these energy centres are the closest points, on our human body manifestation, to the Divine Cosmos, kind of just blew my mind. I have previously understood that the chakra system was important, but had never comprehended it in the way that I do now, anyway I just wanted to share that with you as I hope that you have just had your mind blown as well.

Divining tools are items that we can use to allow us insight to divine wisdom, spiritual guidance, even messages from loved ones that are no longer on the earth plane. There are so many that I could not possibly list them all, so let us just try to group some.

Cards – We have Tarot cards, that most people are aware of, there are Oracle cards, which many people are aware of as well, there are runes, all these items, have been designed by man to assist with the divination of the unknown. As I do use oracle cards and Tarot cards sometimes, I will give you a tutorial from my view after this.

"To truly divine, divine information from the Divine Cosmos, you have only to ask, and you shall receive, humanity has for far too long utilised aids in an attempt to divine answers, they are a crutch, a dependency, that allows for the human being, the diviner, to not take responsibility for passing on the correct information that is required to be passed on."

Another pearler (a profound statement) from our guide. That being said, I will still let you know what to do and how these tools work for me, but we will definitely cover off on the best way of divining messages at the end of this chapter.

With all Tarot and Oracle cards, and I believe Divining Runes, if they are new, they do come with instructions. These instructions give you the information on how to lay the tools out, an understanding of each of the cards or runes, and some even talk a little about divining answers.

FIND IT, THE NEXT STEP IN YOUR SPIRITUAL HEALTH

When I first started using Tarot and Oracle cards, I would be reading the instruction manual for the way to lay out the cards, what each card meant by itself and what it meant in that position. It was not until I started to trust my gut, my instincts, that I really began to progress. I stopped reading the instruction manuals, I still read what the cards meant, sometimes, other times I knew I was being guided. After a while, different items on the cards would standout for me, and I found that if I asked the person, I was doing the reading for, if it had meaning for them, most of the time it did. Now, I just use feeling, intuition, guidance, whatever you want to name it, I will spread the cards in the way I am guided, with an understanding of the placement's meanings, whether that be past, present, future, love, life, whatever. Then we will read the cards meanings together, and then I give them an explanation from the way I understand the cards. Remember to inform whoever you are doing the reading for that this is a guide only, and that they should do more research. The more you use these the better you become.

Dowsing Pendulum – This is simple to use, easy to understand, and can be used for conformation of things that you may not be sure or clear on. You can either buy a pendulum or make one. A pendulum is a weighted item on the end of a tether. A paperclip tied to a piece of cotton will work, a ring and string or chain, necklace, a crystal on a string, basically anything that will swing when you hold it in your fingers.

With the pendulum in hand, you can stand, but I prefer to sit with my elbow supported on a table, ask your higher self to show you a "Yes" answer, and wait. The pendulum after a few seconds may swing, left to right, forward and backwards, diagonally, or in a circle, it may also take longer than a few seconds. Then you ask to be shown a "No" answer, again wait to be shown. I will sometimes ask to show me an "unclear" or "unknown" answer.

Once you know what the pendulum will do for the answers, ask away. I find that I will ask simple questions first, that I know the answers to, this allows me to make sure that it is in tune with me. I normally do not use this method anymore, but some may find it useful.

There are many other divining tools out there, crystal balls, candles, anything that allows your mind to focus, and if you feel you need to use them, please try, research for yourself.

Let us get back to the "ask and you shall receive" part ok.

With your ability to connect with your higher self, communicate, and listen, you no longer require any divining tools. You simply need to ask your higher self for the information you are looking for and then listen for the answers.

I remember when I was learning about this, I did get it very wrong the first few times. It was not until a very good friend of mine gave me some guidance, that I began to understand.

We were sitting together one day and I asked her, when she was giving a reading for someone, how she worked out what the messages meant, the ones that she would get from her higher-self. Her reply was that she did not, she passed the information onto the person who was receiving the reading.

She let me practice on her, I asked spirit if there was any guidance or information that I could pass onto my friend. I ended up seeing a lot of information, worked out what I thought it meant, and gave her my understanding of it.

Afterwards, she quizzed me on how I had come up with that information, I explained that it was my interpretation of the information that spirit had shown me. She then asked me what information I had seen to come to this explanation. So, I started to describe the information that

I was given, during this I remember telling her that I had been shown a building with a flat roof, but did not understand the meaning of it, so I had not included that in my explanation. I also informed her that I had been shown a human figure, in a doorway, I knew it was a man and he was on fire, I did not include this as I could not work out why spirit would show me someone on fire.

Upon hearing this my friend explained to me that many years ago she lived in a building with a flat roof, and her partner at the time was a fireman. This gave a completely different meaning to the reading for her.

Let us drive this point home, shall we. When you are passing on information from spirit, pass on everything, not just the bits that you think the other person will understand, everything!!!

You are given access to information to assist others in finding their way, the information is pertinent to them, let them know what has been passed on.

The next topic I have only recently started to understand, this has taken my whole life to finally get to the understanding that I now have, hopefully I will explain it well enough for you to be able to use it now, and not sometime in the future.

REQUESTING

An act of asking politely or formally for something. This is our description of this word from the dictionary. Note that it does not say ask, it says asking politely, graciously, civilly, courteously, respectfully, or formally, officially, properly, lawfully, correctly. There is a very good reason for this point, so please keep this at the forefront of your mind.

If you recall in chapter 3, we started discussing how some people can just pray or ask for things, and somehow it just turns up in their lives. Others, appear to have the "Midas touch," most things they work on succeed, whilst others still, cannot seem to catch a break.

There is a huge difference in results that people are getting in their lives; would you like to understand why?

This was the basic conclusion in a bite size chunk, that we came to prior to working on communication. As long as what we are requesting is in line with our higher self's spiritual purpose, our true life's path, it strengthens our internal belief system, which, as long as our communication channels, both internal and spiritual, are clear, we should be capable of manifesting whatever we request, or our hearts desire.

This is the information a guide imparted to us on the chakra system.

"The Chakra system is simply the points at which divine energy has the closest contact to the physical form that we are manifesting on this plane. When we become aware of these points of contact, and are able to strengthen them, we are not only able to rectify or enhance our physical being, but also attract a much stronger ability of manifestation, related to each point."

With these three main points established, 1 Requesting, 2 internal beliefs, 3 access to divine energy for manifestation, we are now going to tie together everything you have read, from this book, up until now.

As long as we request in the correct way, that which we truly believe will happen, we are able to manifest or make manifest, our request on earth.

The big sticking point here for many is definitely the belief part, I have tried this so many times throughout my life. The power of positive thinking, think big and grow rich, and many other books I have read, all talk about positive thinking and belief. I was sure I was doing everything correctly.

If we think about the people, we know who pray to get things in their life, or have the "Midas Touch" in the things they do, you will notice one big difference between the unsuccessful and them. They have belief, it is not the belief that I had after reading those books, it is not the belief that we force upon our self-conscious, it is a belief in their heart, that what needs to happen, will happen.

Did I just say heart, I was meant to say Chakra, more precisely, the heart Chakra.

The heart Chakra is positioned at the centre of the Chakra system, making it a central focal point for divine energy, it is the key, the activator, the doorway, the entry point of divine energy to our plane. Once this is accepted and understood, it allows us to envisage that energies flow from the other chakras, to the heart chakra to allow manifestation to occur.

Remember that your request should be in line with your higher self, or your life purpose, therefore, you should have no problem feeling this request in your heart, heart Chakra. This is the part that I had been missing most of my life. Having the belief in your heart that it will happen. This is the one big difference between the successful and the unsuccessful, the people with blind faith, who receive whatever they request and the blind, I mean the rest of us.

For this exercise you should talk with yourself, your spiritual self, it is essential that you work out what is required in your life right now, to assist with your life path or your higher self's spiritual path, it may be big, it may be small, it may even be huge, and you may think that there is no way this will happen. Once you have it, once you know what is required, request of your higher- self, a time, when it is needed by. Is it today, in the next 10 minutes, in the next week, find out when?

Once you understand what is required, and the time frame, you will request, of your higher self, the guidance you need to manifest this, in the time specified.

When I first understood this, I was driving a truck down a highway. Just jokingly, I said in my heart that I would see a pink elephant on the side of the road, I felt it in my heart, in my mind I could see the divine energies emanating from my heart chakra. Then I thought, I really should not mess around, just in case. Less than two minutes later I passed a very large sign of a pink elephant on the side of the road. I believe this was my higher-self proving a point.

1. Request. You know how to be polite, respectful, and humble.

2. Believe. If it has come from your higher-self you had better believe.

3. Listen. Listen for the divine energy, see, feel, hear, or know, your divine spot.

Happy manifesting.

This is like anything else, you have done in his book, the more you practice the better you will become, and understand.

How Do You View the World?

Most of us view the world in a similar manner, understanding that many of us have grown up in societies that enforce education on the children of that society, dictate what should and should not be learnt by the children, and install a working-class system of living, closely resembling slavery, to said society.

That is a bit rough, straight out of the box, don't you think?

Mabey if we break a few things down, it will not seem as glum.

We are born, our parents or guardians, provide shelter, food, in most cases love, the basic understanding of a language, clothing, things to keep us occupied (toys), some even receive religious direction, and basic life lessons, if you do that you will get hurt – if you do this you will get rewarded.

We learn the so-called basics of life, walking, running, being happy, being sad, everything in between, how to make friends, how to make enemies, how to brush our teeth, how to keep our bodies clean.

We go to school. We are taught more about social interaction on a larger scale, educated on the topics that the society has selected for us to learn, we have a reward system taught to us, do well and get an "A" or a pass, do bad and receive an "F" or fail.

Throughout our school life we are exposed to fear and greed on a scale that none of us had comprehended previously. Fear of failing, fear of losing, fear of being different, fear of missing out. We are taught by society at home, school, media, to want the better things in life, best bag, shoes, hair, things. This is where we start to see a hierarchy system come into play, we learn to respect people for what they have, not necessarily for who they are. We are exposed to more religion, maybe the same as what we have learnt at home, maybe different. Most of us learn what that society wants us to learn.

Then we start our working life. We learn that if we are productive in our job, we will receive a reward, payment for our efforts, money. We have learnt about money in our schooling, we learnt that to get the things that make us stand out from the others, we require money. We have been taught that money is real, it is necessary to live. You require money for shelter, food, clothing, transportation, having fun, basically anything in our life requires money.

We work to support ourselves, then our families, all the time being bombarded by society to want the best new things in our life, as this apparently will make our lives better. Everything costs money; therefore, money is real, or so society has taught us.

When we are too old to work, we can retire, but we still require money to live, so unless we have saved enough during our lives, or have succeed in a business or investment, we may still require an income to support our lifestyle.

This still looks sad to me, how about you?

How about we look at it from a different perspective.

We are born.

We go to school.

We get a job.

We build a business. We employ people to work in our business, they do a fantastic job, and the profits increase. The Government of that society requires us to pay them some of the profits (taxes), as we are taking money from the society.

We do this and we see that the money that we have paid to the Government, along with other businesses, has been put towards improving the transport infrastructure of our society. This allows us to expand our business, employ more people from our society and other societies in different regions.

Our company makes more profits, is taxed more by our government and the other societies Governments.

We decide that if we sell our business now, we can retire and not have to work for money for the rest of our lives, so we sell, and get taxed on the amount we sold the business for.

We go off and live a great life, not having to concern ourselves with money, as we have all we could ever need, while our employees, the ones who made our business successful, keep working until they are old enough to retire.

So, in this scenario, we become financially successful, which will probably affect our close family and maybe a friend or two, but the people that did the work, that made the business successful do not have a change in their life.

Maybe we should look at how most people view the world every day, surely that must be better, right?

We wake up, we think about what the day will bring, we go outside into nature and meditate, cleanse our aura, ground ourselves, ask our higher selves if there is anything, we should be aware of or focused on, then we have breakfast where we plan how we can be beneficial to our neighbours, friends, humanity, and the planet.

Hang on, that is how I wished my day started.

Wake up and complain about having to go to our job, or that we do not have a job. Drive or take public transport to our place of work, complaining about, or abusing others, that do not even consider our existence as they are oblivious, along the way. Do what needs to be done at our job so we can be paid money, that will allow us to pay our bills, rent or mortgage, food, etc. All the while being bombarded with advertisements, for the newest things that of course everybody needs.

I am depressed again.

Just look at the life you live at the moment. Now that you have established contact with your higher self, you will be able to see what is not serving your best interests in your life at this time. Be honest with yourself and locate the things that you can do without. The Anger. The Judgment. The Jealousy. The Belittlement. The Fear. The Greed.

When you have found them, you are going to do the first exercise that you learnt in the first book "Fix It."

If you have too many, just do them one at a time, and rectify them all step-by step. This is how I laid this exercise out in the first book, so in case you have not read it and you are still unsure of your higher self just use any of the 1st three. For those who have Identified their higher self, go to number 4.

1. Say a daily affirmation that will ground you as an individual and allow you to succeed in a step-by step, day-by-day process. "I am in control of my own life in every way and I do not need, nor do I wish to _____ (Fill in the gap) today." (Get angry at other drivers, may be good to start with)

2. Say a prayer to God that will ground you as an individual and allow you to succeed in a step-by step, day-by-day process. "God, I call upon your strength as I am back in charge of my life in every way and I do

FIND IT, THE NEXT STEP IN YOUR SPIRITUAL HEALTH

not need, nor wish to _____ (Fill in the gap) today. Amen" (Pass judgment on others, maybe good as well)

3. Ask your angels for the help that you need, to ground you and allow you to succeed in a step by-step, day-by-day process. "I call upon my Archangel to bring me the strength I need as I am back in charge of my life in every way and I do not need, nor do I wish to _____ (Fill in the gap) today." (Be fearful, is something most of us should say)

4. Request of your higher self to allow you to see the spirit in humanity, let your higher-self know what you are attempting to eliminate from your life, anger, belittlement, judgment, fear, all of them or others that you have found.

I use to be an angry driver, I would get mad at other drivers who did not indicate, crossed a solid line, used their phone while driving, basically anything that according to our rules of the road, is deemed illegal. When I looked at the way I viewed this part of my world, I understood that I was being judgemental, I was making that person in control of that vehicle wrong and this would cause anger within me.

When I asked to see the spirit in humanity, I really did not know what I was asking for, but when I drove next, I understood. Now when I drive and a driver does something illegal, I see a loving spirit being, in my divine spot, struggling with its connection to the human being in the vehicle, I sense the oblivion that the human is in, and now instead of anger, I feel love, love for the spirit, when you experience this love, there is no need to forgive anything.

Just by changing how I viewed this part of my world, has made a dramatic difference to how I drive, my blood pressure, and my calmness.

What will happen when you change your view?

In my explanation of things in this chapter I mentioned money and the fact that society enforces money as something real, I will cover more on this in the last chapter of this book.

For now, think about how you would like to be treated.

How Would You Like to be Treated?

If you were asked, how would you like to be treated? You could probably throw out a few words, such as, with respect, as a good person, but maybe nothing too deep.

This is what we are going to look at right now. I would suggest pen and paper, a tablet, computer, or a phone, to allow you to record the information you are about to retrieve.

After reading this next part I would like you to take the time to search for the answers to the above question, not yet, but when I instruct you to.

How would I like to be treated?

I would like to be respected as a spiritually connected human being, who holds love for every other being, human, plant, animal, or other.

I would like to be told my flaws, by my higher self, and other beings, who can see them, to allow me to improve myself as a being.

I would love to be loved for who I am being, for the things that I do to improve others' lives, and spiritual connections.

I would like to be seen as an important figure in the spiritual awakening that is taking place on our planet.

Now that I have established how I would like to be treated; I will take action.

Treat others as you would have them treat you.

In other words, I will now start treating everyone the way I would like to be treated.

All you are required to do now, is to contact your higher self and request guidance on how you would like to be treated. Take your time, feel the connection in your divine spot, allow the information to permeate your being, when you feel, you are ready to write down how you would like to be treated, request that your higher-self assist with the articulation, and write.

There are no right or wrong answers here.

What you write, you write.

This is the first time I have done this exercise, so what you are reading is my very first list of how I would like to be treated. I have been guided to explain that this can be done every few months, as there are things that may be added or that may not serve how we are being, at a particular time in the future.

There will be many challenges in taking these on but remember that it is the journey that counts. Experience and grow as a being, both human and spiritual.

To treat someone who has harmed or wronged you with love or respect is a very difficult thing to do, therefore, if this comes up as a part of your answers, remember to detach, and view that person's higher self as your point of interaction.

If it ends up being just me who follows this step the world will still be a better place, if one other is inspired to follow this step, the world will be an even better place. What do you think the world would look like if 100 people took this step on, or 1000 people, or a multitude more?

I was at a music festival recently, one of the first to take place after the Covid 19 lock down in my area. I was part of the crew looking after the ablutions (toilets, showers, handwash, and hand sanitisers), so we interacted with many of the festival goers.

Most of the patrons I can honestly say were living the way I have explained in this chapter, they were thoughtful, caring, considerate, and full of love and joy. They were treating everyone as they themselves would like to be treated. I had never experienced a festival like it in my life.

My point with this story is that even without us doing anything in this chapter there are already people who are living this way, they are happy, joyful, full of love, and a pleasure to be around. That is the feeling I will be leaving with the people in my life from now on.

Healing Yourself and Others

When we feel good about ourself, It is easier to feel good about others, within this book so far, we have only covered matters that relate to our spiritual health, what we must address now is related to our spiritual health, but many are not aware of it.

Our body is our temple, what we bring into our temple dictates how effective our connection with the Divine Cosmos will be. If we feed the body crap, with no thought into the nutrition that we are introducing, or not introducing, then we can create problems. If we sit on our bum and do not consider exercise to increase our blood flow throughout the vital parts of our bodies, again we can create problems.

This is not a diet book or an exercise program, and I do not want it to be. I would just like you to have access to some very basic food and exercise information, if you already know this, fantastic, if not, you are welcome.

I am not a nutritionist, so the following information is only general, you should seek out a qualified professional if you believe you require further advice.

Nutritious food is not full of sugar, or full of carbohydrates. It is normally natural food, the likes of fresh meat, chicken, beef, pork, fish, if you are a meat eater all these proteins are fine. If you are a vegetarian or vegan, you still require protein, so, you can now get "not meats," these are things that may resemble meats, like bacon, chicken, and beef, but are made from plant proteins. You can also just utilise plant protein.

Then we do require a source of good, or complex carbohydrates and fibre. We can get this from vegetables the likes of broccoli, carrots, cauliflower, beans, peas, and the list goes on. I would suggest limiting the high starch vegetables, such as potatoes and rice, you do not need to avoid them maybe just do not have them every day.

FIND IT, THE NEXT STEP IN YOUR SPIRITUAL HEALTH

Salads are good, just limit or avoid the dressings.

Eggs are fine, in case you do not know, the egg whites are protein, and the yokes have carbohydrates.

Breads are normally high in carbs, so just look for the higher protein ones, and limit the ones that are high in carbs.

Sweets, cookies, cakes, pastries, and the like are normally full of sugar, but you can get the sugar free alternatives. Be mindful of the sugar substitute that is used.

If you look at the following list of names, they are all names for sugar, look on the labels of some of the items that you buy, you will find many of these on them. I remember buying a brand of fruit roll ups for my children, it was not until I read the label at home that I realised it had at least 4 different types of sugar in them. I never bought those again. They were advertised as containing real fruit, but were made of over 50% sugar.

Barley malt, Barbados sugar, Beet sugar, Brown sugar, Buttered syrup, Cane juice, Cane sugar, Caramel, Corn syrup, Corn syrup solids, Confectioner's sugar, Carob syrup, Castor sugar, Date sugar, Dehydrated cane juice, Demerara sugar, Dextran, Dextrose, Diastatic malt, Diastase, Ethyl maltol, Free flowing brown sugars, Fructose, Fruit juice, Fruit juice concentrate, Galactose, Glucose, Glucose solids, Golden sugar, Golden syrup, Granulated sugar, Grape sugar, High fructose corn syrup, Honey, Icing sugar, Invert sugar, Lactose, Malt, Maltodextrin, Maltose, Malt syrup, Mannitol, Maple syrup, Molasses, Muscovado, Panocha, Powdered sugar, Raw sugar, Refiner's syrup, Rice syrup, Sucrose, Treacle, Turbinado sugar, Yellow sugar.

Some of these sugars are absorbed by our bodies easier than normal sugar, all I am saying is just be aware.

You can find more information on line on these topics, I would probably suggest not asking family and friends for information, unless they are nutritionists.

Exercise, this one is simple, just move vigorously, if you cannot run, then walk until you are able to run, if you cannot walk, move the parts of your body that you are able to, get your blood moving. Our human bodies are not designed to be sedentary; we require movement to keep them healthy, and our blood needs to move through our various organs to filter out disease.

If we are looking after our physical body, it will also enhance our spiritual connection, when they are both working well together, much of the energy work that we have gone through in the first few chapters, will automatically assist our physical body.

Now that your connection with your higher self is in place, you can request guidance for creating the physical being that you desire, try it, see what information you get in return. It will be the truth but you must make the decision to use it or not.

Healing yourself, here are a few ways of conducting healing on your own body. Remember that you should also seek medical advice as soon as possible for any serious ailment.

A. If you have a cut, graze, a superficial wound, we all know that we should apply pressure. When you do this, you can use your spiritual connection to bring in extra healing. Just sense in your Divine spot, that there is divine energy flowing through your chakras, into your body, and to the point of the injury.

B. If the wound requires medical involvement, you can firstly alleviate much of the pain by connecting with your higher self and requesting assistance. During and after the medical involvement, you can do the same as explained in A. this will assist in faster healing times.

C. If there is sickness in or on the body, you should seek medical advice as well as advice from your higher self. A doctor will normally be able to tell you what the sickness is and how he/she believes it can be treated. Your higher self, can inform you what it is, why you have it and how you can eliminate it. For the best results, listen to both. I myself have rarely been sick, I have been injured, but rarely has sickness of the body affected me.

D. This is a continuation of c. as our guide would like to add in this. "You now have divine access via your higher-self; therefore, you have access to both lost and new knowledge, cures and medical solutions to ailments that still baffle your medical professionals. You may be able to guide your medical professional to a solution for your treatment, if not, along with your medical treatment, you may access a psychic surgeon. This is done via you higher-self, you will need to request a psychic surgeon to rectify the human body ailment. If this is granted it can be rather draining, both physically and spiritually, but extremely effective."

Healing others. When we feel confident with our ability in our own healing, we can do the same for others. This can be done with physical touch, without physical touch, and even remotely, meaning we could be at home and use divine energy healing on someone in another country.

As we now understand that the closest points on a person's body to divine energy is via their chakras, you only require to direct the divine energy via that person's chakras, to the affected area. You are not sending the energy from yourself, but directing the energy from the Divine Cosmos via their chakras. You can conduct cleansings, groundings, place protection, and balance another person's chakras, whilst with them or remotely.

I have only touched on some of the things that you are capable of undertaking as far as healing yourself and others, as you will gain more information and a better understanding via your higher-self.

What Happens When We Die?

When our human being stops being, when our body ceases to function, what happens?

When I was 15 years old my father passed away, in his bed, at our home. He had been a very sick man for the last 2 years of his life, he had renal failure (acute kidney failure), one of his kidney's was the size of his little finger nail and the other was none existent. We had a dialysis machine in one of the bedrooms of our home, that my mother would hook him up to it, 2 to 3 times each week.

I came home from school one day to find my mother crying in the kitchen and my fathers' doctor in the lounge room talking with my father. My mother explained that the doctor had just told my father that he estimated my father would only live, at most, 6 more months.

That night before going to bed, my two younger sisters and I all gave our father a hug and told him we loved him.

My older brother was seated at the end of my bed later that night, shaking me from my sleep gently, and saying he had something to tell me.

I recall sitting up in my bed, looking at my brother, and saying Dad's dead isn't he.

What my brother did not realise was that he had woken me from a very vivid dream. In the dream my father had been seated on a large log made of clouds, he looked younger, and healthier than I had ever remembered seeing him in human life. The emotion from his face was beaming joy and happiness as he looked out at all his lost relatives and friends from this life.

I got out of my bed, walked to my father's room, and looked at his body lying motionless in his bed, I knew that my father was fine and happy in the place that I had just seen him, and that his body was just a shell, not him.

"This is a lesson that many generations, throughout the centuries, have been striving to understand, and at this present state on the earth plane I believe the answer is able to ring true in most human beings' hearts."

"The Divine Cosmos is everything, everything that we understand, everything that we do not understand, and everything that we do not know exists. The Divine Cosmos is for the human brain, beyond comprehension, so humanity has grouped it into the meaning of the word God.

Our higher-self is a part of the Divine Cosmos and our higher-self is our true self, even though most of humanity views our physical being as our true self.

When your human body ceases being, you become aware of yourself as your higher-self in the Divine Cosmos, you are no longer bound by being human, the concept of time, which is the vail on the earth plane, disappears, and is replaced by an evolving consciousness of all things. We are all interconnected beings, we are connected by the Divine Cosmos, to each other and everything.

All your knowledge from your experience of being human is retained, you as your higher-self, expand your spiritual being with every experience you gain from the earth plane and the other planes of existence."

There is far too much to explain in detail within this book, but the glimpse of an explanation that we have received is but the very tip of the iceberg.

You may want to request this information for yourself from one of your own guides, as it is very possible that you will receive more in-depth information that will assist with your understanding of this topic.

When I requested this information, I was shown the part of our ego dying with our human body, I became a little upset as I thought that the ego was me, and that the ego was my being. I was guided to understand that our ego is like the operational system for a computer, it has hard wired programming to keep our being functioning without any input from our higher-selves.

Now that we know what we know, what is it that we should be doing.

Every experience that we have is retained and our higher-self expands with every experience. Therefore, our goal is to experience as much as possible, to live life, to experience everything that we can.

Now would be a very good time to converse with your higher-self, find out what other things you may be required to experience, find out your true-life path, find out what is in store for you.

If fear and money were not of issue to you, what would you be driven to experience in this life?

How Do You Want Your World to Look?

Part of the journey I have ahead of me involves everybody who reads these "It" books, including the next one that I have been informed, I will be writing.

Many of you are now coming to grips with your spirituality, your connection to your higher-self, and the Divine Cosmos. We all have access to divine energies that can be used to fix so many things in our world, that have been considered too difficult, of no real importance, or not practical.

I mentioned back in chapter 7, that I would continue with what I was alluding to about society enforcing that money is real. I will have that conversation soon but first I would like to explain why I believe we must have this conversation.

If you are not already aware, we now live in a world that is controlled by just a handful of individuals, they control, Countries, although most are not Royalty, Presidents, or Heads of State. They Control companies, although most are not on the board of directors, or the company owners, they control society, through a system that they have perverted. They believe that they are entitled, that it is their right, to rule the world.

To save this planet for us all, this earth plane, it is this perversion, deception, these lies, that we must eliminate.

There are beautiful things to come in our future, but for them to happen we need the change to start now. In the last 'It' book, Fix It, we learnt some spiritual basics, and left you with hope. In this 'It' book, Find It, you have connected with your higher-self on a level of a spiritual warrior, you are now going to take the action to allow this change to start. It will not happen overnight, it does not need to, but it needs to start.

For some, this next bit of information will not come as a shock, as you already understand, but like most human beings, have not been unable to find an alternative, for others it will be a shock, and others yet, will not believe, to this last group – ask your higher-self for conformation.

We have all been sold into slavery to these handful of people via a massive lie, that lie is money. Money has not been worth the paper, or metal that it is printed on for about fifty years now, maybe longer.

The world's economy is controlled by a few individuals, that have managed to get the world to believe that this money is real. It is all credit based, maybe there is one country that still has its currency backed by gold, the rest are all credit based, all in debt, or owned by these individuals.

They control the marketing, they play on our ego's needs, they focus on the basic earth desires, instead of the requirements of the higher-self, which creates obstacles for our divine connection. The more belief we install into this lie, the stronger they become.

We will change this, in a step-by-step, day-by-day system, now we only need to work out- How do you want your world to look?

When we do this last exercise, I would like you to connect with your higher-self first and request to know your basic needs, personally, for your neighbourhood, for your city, for your county and for your world.

I will show you what I would like my world to look like first, and then, I would like you to do what I show you, but for you, for your world.

Personally –

1. I would like a home of my own, just the basics, no more, a place where I can relax, have family and friends over.

2. I would like an electric vehicle.

3. I would like to ensure that I do not have a carbon foot print, in fact I would like to remove carbon from the air of our planet each year instead of adding to it.

4. I would like to not have to worry about money.

5. I would like to contribute to my family, friends, neighbours, and society, in a positive way every day.

6. I would like to eat nutritious food every day.

7. I would like clean, presentable clothes.

8. I would like to travel, visit friends in different cities, countries and visit new countries.

9. I would like time to meditate and connect with my higher-self.

My community –

1. I would like to have pleasant neighbours, that talk to each other.

2. I would like a neighbourhood garden.

3. I would like access to facilities in my neighbourhood, swimming pool, gym, green areas, etc.

4. I would like it to be safe.

My Town/City –

1. I would like it to have less traffic.

2. I would like the traffic to be majorly electric.

3. I would like it to be safe.

4. I would like to go to shops and everything that I needed was free, or I could barter with items I had.

5. I would like for everyone to have the time to get to know each other.

6. I would like free transport.

My Country -

1. I would like it to be self-sufficient, producing everything that its citizens require.

2. I would like a real say in how it is run, not just a choice between bad options.

3. I would like it to be a shinning, positive example to other countries, by eliminating carbon output, and increasing carbon absorption.

4. I would like it to help its own citizens and those of less fortunate countries.

5. I would like it to be safe.

My World –

1. I would like it to be clean.

2. I would like it to be safe.

3. I would like it to be equal opportunity for everyone, not a race, not a competition, but equal. Everyone has shelter, food, clothing, love, care, fun.

4. I would like it to be repaired, no more melting polar ice caps, no more crazy weather, no more environmental disasters.

5. I would like everyone to have access to their higher-selves.

FIND IT, THE NEXT STEP IN YOUR SPIRITUAL HEALTH

Some of the things on my personal list I have now, some I know I can get later; I know that I can achieve all of them, if I believe.

The rest will take some work, they would be achieved a lot faster if I did not need to go to work, to make money, to pay my bills, so that I can afford to pay for my house, food, insurance, etc.

As you can see, this is where most of us end up, at the moment it is very difficult to do much more than look after yourself and your loved ones, and sometimes even that is a challenge.

I will let you know what I am being guided to do soon, but right now, please put this book down, contact your higher-self, and write your list.

List.

List.

List.

List.

List.

Ok then, your lists are done, that is fantastic.

I bet some of you have not done them, go on, help yourself out, write them down.

You probably found, that by connecting with your higher-self, your personal list is nowhere near as long as it would be if you allowed your ego to write the list, if ego wrote it, then it would probably include things like diamond rings and boats, right.

First things first, for those of you who have written down that you want your own garden, or even if you already have your own garden now, or you have any produce, I would like you to find a local café, shop, bakery, anything, and set up a barter system with them. Just something small, a bag of tomatoes for a coffee, or a dozen eggs for a couple of loaves of bread.

Using items that the earth has produced for you to get an item in leu of money. So, remember you do not want the money, it is not real, you cannot drink or eat it.

If you want to reduce your carbon foot print, you could go solar on your house, buy an electric vehicle, or plant a garden, that would grow veggies, that would remove carbon from the air, that you can eat, and use some for barter.

I hope you are getting the point, just start doing small things, if we all start doing these small things, it makes a difference. First 10 people, then 100, then 1,000, and so on.

The next 'It' book will be on environmental solutions for ourselves, our neighbourhoods, Towns or Cities, and maybe the countries and the world, we will see if I can get them in, if not there will be an 'It" book number 4, I guess.

I was saying before that I am being guided to do something, I will explain a bit about it now, and more so in the next "It" book.

In the first book, I mentioned an inventor who had an amazing influence on me, with his inventions, business structure and view of the world. Unfortunately, a couple of years ago he passed on, left this plane of existence.

I now have been guided to begin manifesting some land, for an Economy Building Community, that I will assist in constructing, with my inventor friends higher-self.

FIND IT, THE NEXT STEP IN YOUR SPIRITUAL HEALTH

When my friend and I first discussed this Idea, a few years ago, it was because we saw so many retirees, getting the short end of the stick. They were told when they could retire by our government and many could not survive on the pension, so they tried to keep working, but were told, by society, that they were too old.

Our plan was simple, some land, make it self-sufficient, generate its own power, with the excess being sold back onto the grid, treat its own sewerage and waste, turning the un-usable into usable supplies.

Set up Micro – Businesses, that would be community run, and of benefit to the community.

Affordable housing, nothing fancy, but the basics, and community facilities.

The basic idea was the that a person would join the community, more as a business partner, they would share in the work, as well as the profits, and the living expenses would be covered by the community.

I will be explaining a lot more about this in the next book, my plan is to make it a bit like a blueprint, that can be copied, duplicated in other areas. Remember we need to take care of our elders and other vulnerable people within our societies.

I know there will be a lot more to come, If I am to work with my friends higher-self, it should make for an interesting ride.

For now, please stay connected to your higher-self, use divine healing on yourself and others.

Be guided by what is in your heart, and use your head, do not be guided by your head.

Keep clean and stay close to the Divine Cosmos.

With love and light.

Also by Desmond Knipe

FIX IT
FIX IT, A basic guide to your spiritual health
FIND IT, the next step in your spiritual health